STENCILLING
ON FABRICS

STENCILLING ON FABRICS

Wren Loasby

Broadcast Books

British Library Cataloguing in Publication Data

Loasby, Wren
   Stencilling on fabrics.
   I. Title
   745.73

ISBN 1854040073

Published by Broadcast Books Ltd
The Old School House
The Courtyard
Bell Street
Shaftesbury
Dorset
SP7 8BP

Printed in Hong Kong.

Contents

Introduction

In recent years there has been a great resurgence in the very ancient craft of stencilling. People began to realise that they could create their own unique decorative schemes by using a stencil imaginatively. Walls decorated with lively stencilling can now be seen everywhere, from the simplest cottage to the grandest of houses.

It is not only walls which can benefit from stencilling; it is an extremely versatile form of decoration and can be used equally well on floors, ceilings and furniture. However, for anyone seeking something truly unique in their decorative scheme then stencilling on fabric must be one of the easiest ways of producing the most fabulous results. The purpose of this book is to show how even ordinary materials can be lifted into something quite special by the use of judicious stencilling.

The step-by-step photographs on pages 14 and 15 and the pictures of finished items produced from basic stencils should encourage and, hopefully, inspire even the most faint-hearted to try the techniques described. You will go from strength to strength as you appreciate the vast potential you have, literally, at your fingertips. Not only can straightforward fabrics be decorated, but think about the possibilities of producing quilted bedheads with matching bedspreads, pretty curtain tie-backs, stencilling a plain roller blind to add interest, or even creating your own tapestry canvases.

There are many stencils available but it is much more fun to create your own. Many of the stencils used on the articles in this book are reproduced on the following pages for you to cut for yourself. If you do not want to cut the pages they can be traced directly onto a piece of clear acetate which can then be cut. Alternatively, trace onto a piece of waxed manilla card, which is the traditional stencil material. The joy of these stencils is that all the hard work has been done for you. The strong bridges – which hold the stencil together – are already incorporated so you simply have to cut around the black shapes with a sharp craft knife, an exercise which you should find interesting and which will give you a good 'feel' for the shapes you are producing.

Happy stencilling!

Stencilling on fabrics

Many fabrics and soft furnishing materials can be enhanced by stencilling them with a pattern appropriate to your particular room or needs. The main thing to remember is that the fabric should be fairly closely woven and not have too much surface texture because you want to produce as clean an outline as possible.

All closely-woven furnishing cottons – even as simple as calico or curtain lining – accept a stencil very well and, because they are cheap, can be used lavishly to make very rich-looking curtains or full-length tablecloths. As I mentioned in the introduction, the stiffened fabric used for roller blinds is a particularly suitable medium for stencilling and I have even created large 'rugs' on corded fitted carpet. These work particularly well under, say, a dining table to add emphasis to that area or in hallways to disguise areas of heavy wear where the carpet itself may have become worn or badly marked.

As your confidence increases you will probably move on from the cotton materials and see the possibilities of stencilling onto dupions, linens, or silk. Sheer materials can look very dramatic when stencilled with, say, gold paints, or very ethereal when stencilled in a very delicate shade. One of the prettiest window dressings I have seen was sheer material lightly stencilled with carefully placed 'random' leaves. When the curtains moved in the summer breeze it looked as if leaves were gently drifting in from the sunlit garden, creating a very beautiful effect.

There are now several paints on the market which are suitable for using on fabric. I have used ozone-friendly spray paints to great effect and they withstand washing very well. They are quick to use once you have got the 'feel' of the nozzle control, but the quickness of the actual application is countered by the time you must spend carefully masking the surrounding area of fabric so that it does not pick up the fine mist of colour.

Certainly for anyone starting to stencil on fabric I would recommend the wide range of fabric paints now available. These come in small pots, or in the form of fat felt-tip pens. A combination of brush and pen work can produce spectacular results.

A fat, stubby brush is the traditional stencilling tool, but almost any brush can be used provided the bristles are trimmed to give a flat surface. Ideally you should use a separate brush for each colour so that you can keep up

Cross-stitch rug
This rug has been created by stencilling a series of border designs onto rug canvas and has been worked in rich blue and terracotta shades in the style of an Afghan kelim.

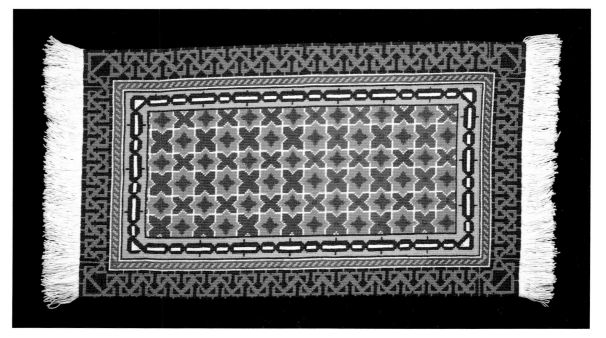

an even flow of work and not have to stop to rinse out one colour before using another. A newly washed brush, however dry you may feel it is, will always retain a little moisture and could, quite literally, produce a water mark or ring around the paint and spoil your work. You will find it useful to have several different sizes of brush – small ones so that you can

Fruit Bowl
Another wall stencil applied to canvas and then worked in rich colours over both the design and the stencil-ties. The background has not been worked so that the design would stand out within a frame. The same design could be made into an attractive cushion cover by working the background in a rich cream or dark green tapestry wool.

Cornucopia
An example of a stencil applied to a tapestry canvas. The stencil-ties have been coloured over to add richness to the overall design.

get into small areas easily and bigger ones for large areas.

With your brushes, paint and a good supply of kitchen roll on hand you are ready to start. First of all decide where you want to place your stencil and then hold it firmly in position with some low-tack masking tape so that it does not move when you are working. If you are going to repeat the stencil several times on one piece of material it is worth taking the time to work out the distance between each repeat and marking it on the fabric with tailor's chalk.

When it comes to actually applying the paint I find it best to shake the bottle of colour well and then use the paint which adheres to the cap itself. You need remarkably little paint on your brush and by using the cap you do not waste any at all. Dip just the tip of the brush into the paint and then stamp it up and down on a piece of kitchen roll to remove the excess. The brush will appear to be almost dry and this is how it should be. Apply the brush to the

fabric with an up and down movement, or by keeping your wrist very flexible and making circular motions with the brush. You will soon find which method you prefer and a few practice runs will help decide. If you have too much paint on the bristles the colour will creep under the edge of the stencil and give a fuzzy outline instead of the crisp edge you are trying to achieve.

It is best to build up the colour gradually and, as a general rule of thumb, more colour should be applied to the edges of the stencil

Tie-backs
The poppy stencil has been adapted to curve and make a stencilled tie-back – see centre – and also put onto tapestry canvas so that the design can be worked in half cross-stitch. For the ivy-leaf tie-back the stencil has been applied to the material which has then been backed with wadding and muslin so that the design can be quilted to produce a rich three-dimensional effect.

than to the centre. This will produce an attractive three-dimensional effect which can be further enhanced by perhaps adding just a touch of another colour on top of the main shade.

When you have completed your chosen design leave the paint a little while to completely dry and then use a hot iron on the wrong side of the fabric to press and set the colour. I am sure you will be delighted with the results and, like me, will soon be looking around for your next project!

Table cloth and cushion

An elegant poppy design is used to great effect on this circular tablecloth. The stencil has been applied eight times at regular intervals around the cloth and a simple circlet of poppy buds is used in the centre. The same motif has been used to create a matching cushion.

Baby Quilt

Repetitions of the Flump stencil have been used here to great effect on a baby's quilt. The Teddy and Goose stencils make the bibs something special.

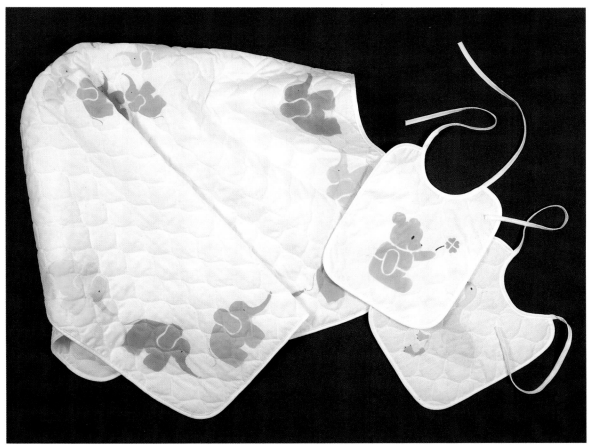

The Wren Design

Before going any further let us take a look at the way in which the various stencil designs on the following pages might be used on different fabrics.

The Wren stencil shown on page 1 is my business logo and I have used it many times to show the sheer versatility of one stencil design. For instance, at its most basic it makes an attractive letterhead but just look what can be done with the same design when it is used on various fabrics.

When exhibiting at a trade show I decided to stencil some cotton T-shirts with my logo, using a shade of green similar to that used on my letterhead and you can see the result on page 13.

Next, because I am a keen needlewoman, I decided to stencil it onto some 10-holes-to-the-inch tapestry canvas to see if I could turn it into a wall-hanging. I used only a soft brown fabric paint to lightly colour the canvas and then, ignoring the stencil 'ties', used various shades of brown and cream to reproduce the myriad shadings found in the garden wren.

Encouraged by the results of this my next project was to use the design again, together with the ivy corner shown on page 31, and this time I worked it in shades of blue to complement the furnishings of a particular room, working the background as well to make a cushion cover.

By now it had become a challenge to see what else could be done with the design, so the next project was to stencil it onto plain calico. Using the ties as guidelines, I quilted around the shapes with matching silks and then decided to add further interest by quilting the background in a diamond pattern, using embroidery silk in a neutral cream shade.

Finally, having been given a sweatshirt with a fabric panel across the front, I reduced the design, using a photocopier, and stencilled four wrens across the fabric, which were then worked in silks using a cross-stitch.

The wren just happens to be my logo and I have used it here purely as an example of the versatility of one stencil used on very different fabrics and producing pleasing results every time. I hope it will encourage you to try some of these ideas too, do not forget that all the designs in this book can be enlarged or reduced on a photocopier, two or more designs can be used together to create quite different effects or just one element of a particular design can be 'lifted' and used alone to create something truly unique – the possibilities are only as limited as your own imagination!

Wren Tapestry Cushion
A combination of two stencils used on tapestry canvas and then worked in half cross-stitch makes a unique cushion cover.

Brown Wren
Leftover lengths of wool have been used to work this wall-hanging in half cross-stitch. The unworked background creates a three-dimensional effect.

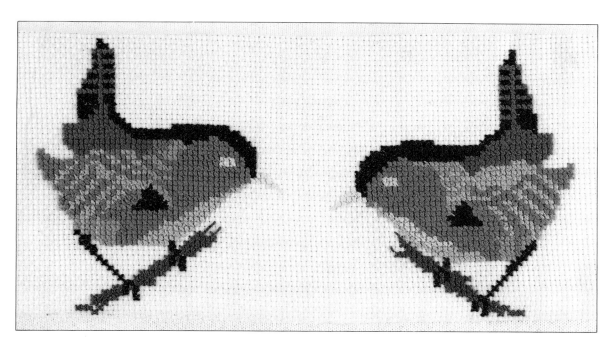

Wren Sweatshirt

The Wren stencil has been reduced and then applied to the even weave insert of the sweatshirt. It looked good just as it was but even better when worked in cross-stitch to match a favourite outfit.

Wren T-shirt

T-shirts are ideal subjects on which to try out fabric stencilling. When the paint is applied with a small sponge instead of a brush this attractive dappled effect can be achieved.

Quilted Wren

An entirely different finish created this time by stencilling some fabric backing it with wadding and muslin and then using a simple quilting stitch to add depth to the design.

Step-by-step

Before applying a stencil to any surface, particularly fabric, try out various colour combinations. Lining paper is cheap to use for this purpose and time spent on a few practice colourways is well worthwhile. When you like a particular colour combination, take a spare piece of your chosen fabric and try it out on that. Remember that the paint will seep into the fabric fibres and give a smoother appearance than your paper 'pattern'.

1 Tracing a design onto stencil card
Start by placing a piece of tracing paper over your chosen design and carefully pencil over the black shapes. When you are satisfied that you have traced everything transfer the tracing onto stencil card by placing a sheet of carbon paper between the tracing and the card. Keep it in place by using a strip of masking tape at the top and bottom of the design. Go over the traced shapes with a ball-point pen, pressing firmly so that all the design is transferred to the stencil card.

2 Blocking-in and cutting out the stencil
Roughly fill in the shape with a soft pencil before starting to cut. This is called 'blocking-in'. Use a cutting board for cutting the stencil. This can be something as simple as an old breadboard or as sophisticated as a professional cutting board. Using a disposable craft knife, cut around the blocked-in shapes. Start at the centre of the design and work outwards. Hold the knife at an angle. This will give a slight bevel to the cut edge and help prevent the paint from creeping. Try to cut smoothly so that jagged edges do not spoil the outline.

3 Trial run with paint and brushes
Fabric paints are available in an extensive range of colours. It is best to have a separate stencil brush for each shade used. To apply paint through a stencil, first dip the brush into the paint and then stamp it up and down on a pad of kitchen paper to remove excess paint. The brush should be virtually dry, and you will find that you need very little to cover quite a large area. Apply the paint through the cut stencil by 'pouncing' the brush up and down, or by using a light circular motion.

4 Applying paint to the fabric

Now you are ready to go 'live' and the first thing to do is to make sure that the fabric is smooth and as taut as possible. Pin it in place if necessary. Position the stencil and hold it in place with masking tape. Apply the paint sparingly, gradually building up the colour to achieve the desired effect. The paint will dry almost immediately.

5 The finished result

Now carefully lift off the stencil and enjoy the thrill of seeing what you have created! If you wish to apply more colour carefully reposition the stencil over the design and apply the paint. Here a garland has been formed by repeating the stencil pattern in the form of a circle.

6 Made up cushion

Press the fabric on the wrong side to 'set' the paint and then make up as required. Here the stencilled design has been simply quilted and made up into a cushion cover.

Butterfly

A simple shape for cutting out, and a design for which I am sure you will find many uses.

It looks particularly good when stencilled onto muslin or sheer curtains as the diaphanous quality of both these fabrics seems to echo the fragile feeling of butterfly wings.

I have used this design, together with a simple bow design, to make a most attractive needlepoint cushion cover. Both shapes lend themselves well to the quilting technique.

Think about stencilling the sets of wings in different colours, or blend two or three complementary shades together – applying one after the other as the paint dries – to give a misty, cloudy effect which can be so pretty.

Fleur de Lys

The Fleur de Lys really is a classic design and I am sure that you will find my version of it easy to cut out and to use.

I first used it stencilled in charcoal grey on a thick white cotton bedspread. With tailor's chalk I drew a diamond-shaped grid over the entire bedspread and then at the intersections I stencilled the Fleur de Lys. The tailor's chalk easily brushed out when the paint was completely dry, and the end result was an unusual and elegant bedspread.

I have also used this design to stencil a shower curtain (using spray paints this time because of the moisture problem) and, in a smaller version, along the top of the shower tiles. It completely transformed the plain white shower curtain and added considerably to the impact of the plain white tiling.

Goosey Gander

Nothing could be simpler to cut out than this goose design and the knife just seems to glide around the easy shape.

Geese look fun marching along in line. If a smaller version is also used it is easy to make a really charming picture of a mother goose accompanied by goslings.

As with all the children's stencils, take the time to add an eye with a fabric felt-tip pen. In the case of this goose just tip the webbed feet with black to suggest claws. Tiny details, but what a difference they make!

Flump

Whenever I doodle I draw 'flumps' so I thought it would be fun to draw a very simple shape to be used in a child's room.

The tail and the trunk line up nicely, so it can be used as a continuous frieze, each flump appearing to hold the other's tail exactly like circus elephants.

Think about enlarging or reducing the design to make a 'family' of flumps, or cut out two so that they can face each other in a variation of the frieze theme.

Finally, don't forget to add a tiny eye. It makes such a difference.

Tile Design

This design itself could not be easier to cut. It is based on a Persian tiled floor, and the recurring motifs looked extremely attractive when used in different blocks of colour to form even more patterns.

The basic design was used as the starting point for the needlework rug shown on page 8. Taking some rug canvas, which had five holes to the inch, I first measured the design and then worked out how many repeats I could get into a rectangle. I stencilled these very lightly onto the canvas as I was not yet sure of the colours I wanted to use. Because I was working on squares which were easy to count I decided to further embellish the basic shapes by working the centres in contrasting wools and used a cream shade to disguise all the stencil 'ties'.

The two elements of this design could be used separately to form a geometric border on the leading edge and bottom of the curtains. Alternatively, think about adapting it to make a 'patchwork' quilt or cushion, colouring the motifs in different shades and then perhaps quilting around them.

Teddy

This teddy design was also used to decorate a cot blanket, using it around the complete border. To add interest I reversed every other teddy so that they appeared both to face each other and sit back-to-back. This can be done easily by turning the stencil over and painting through the other side, or by cutting the shape out twice and using the two stencils alternately.

Two enlarged teddies were placed in the centre of the blanket and a smaller teddy stencilled along the bottom of spotted muslin curtains. Again it looks more balanced if on the left-hand curtain the teddies face towards the right and vice-versa for the right-hand curtain. A small detail, but giving the impression that someone has really thought about using the design well.

Kangaroo

There is something very lovable about the shape of the kangaroo and instead of the more usual bunnies and kittens I thought I would design a kangaroo stencil to be used in a children's room.

This design was enlarged and placed in the centre of a previously quilted cot blanket. Cot bumpers were also stencilled with the slightly smaller design and the baby kangaroo was used to decorate a baby pillow.

Although I have not done it, I feel this design would make an ideal birth sampler where the baby's name and birth date could be added with simple embroidery stitches.

This and the other children's designs in this book would look great fun if stencilled onto plain T-shirts and sweatshirts and would certainly look more individual than any shop-bought design.

At the side of the main design you will see that I have suggested where the eye and eyebrow should be placed to add life to the finished piece. All the children's stencils should have at least one eye added by a fabric pen.

Ivy Corner

This is the stencil which I used on the blue Wren cushion shown on page 12. It is a very adaptable design and could be used in all manner of situations. For instance, in the corners of a table cloth or pillowcase, at the bottom of a curtain to carry the eye along the edges, or to add interest to a plain pelmet.

Most leaves make attractive stencils and for this design I traced around an actual ivy leaf and then placed ties in strategic places to add life to the overall design. Why not try something similar with a prettily-shaped leaf?

Ivy Frieze

This ivy frieze was designed to be used with the ivy corner and the combination of the two can give endless permutations.

On a fabric pelmet I have used the ivy corner at each end and then linked them together with this frieze. The two 'stems' at each end line up with each other and can be used as registration markers. Moving on to the curtains, I stencilled the bottom centre corner of each with the ivy 'corner' and then ran this frieze along the bottom edges and up the leading front edges of each curtain – a very simple but effective method of producing a unique pair of curtains.

As with all the other stencils in this book, do not forget that they can be coloured to match your colour scheme – an ivy leaf does not have to be green, it could be deep blue, red or whatever you like. Adapt it to blend with your other furnishings.

This frieze was also used to make the tie-backs on page 10 and, to give a feeling of luxury, I used a thick wadding between the stencilled fabric and the backing before quilting around the design. It was very quick to do and the result looked very attractive when in place.

Ribbons and Bows

Ribbons and bows must be some of the most appealing subjects around, particularly for those people who like pretty things.

The bow stencil shown here, although basically a corner design, can be adapted in many ways. On a delicate silk cushion cover it could be used in just one corner, on two opposite corners or in each of the four corners. It could look particularly pretty on a lace-edged pillow case.

Not all the flowing 'ribbons' need be stencilled, and when used without the two longer ribbons at each side it would build up into an attractive frieze with the bows placed side-by-side.

Beneath the bow is a simple ribbon which can be used to link the bows. Let your imagination flow freely and see what variations you can come up with for their use on all kinds of fabrics.

Simple Rose

The rose stencil which is used to illustrate the step-by-step techniques on pages 14 and 15 is shown on the opposite page.

It is an easy design to start off with, not only for learning how to cut out a stencil but also because the 'ties' are quite broad. You should find it easy to apply paint to the fabric using medium-sized stencil brushes.

The design is very versatile. It can be used as a single motif to decorate pillow cases, table napkins etc. Alternatively, use it in a line to create a frieze, or in a circle to create the garland effect shown on page 15.

Because of the width of the ties it is ideal for outlining. It gives a quilted effect which works well on cushion covers and bedspreads where the actual mechanics of the quilting technique are hidden by another layer of cloth. Wherever you choose to use it do remember to test the colours on a similar piece of cloth first. Practice the effects you want to achieve before applying the fabric paints to the actual article to be stencilled – once applied it is very difficult to conceal mistakes!

Horn of Plenty

The Horn of Plenty is always a popular design and this one has been simplified to make the cutting easy.

Although one usually associates the Horn of Plenty with fruit tumbling from it, I thought a simple tulip shaped flower could look pretty and delicate. It has the naïve charm of some of the early Pennsylvania Dutch designs.

It looks good scattered on plain but textured curtains, or as a pelmet frieze. I think it would also look attractive in a kitchen and could be used to decorate a tea cosy, oven mitts or squab cushions on kitchen stools.

Fruit

This is a stencil which I designed for someone who wanted to update their kitchen cupboards without going to the expense of having new fitments.

The whole design, coloured in reds, deep golds, apricot and greens, looked well on the larger doors, and the three apples to the right of the design were used on some of the smaller doors. However, the kitchen really came to life when the same design was used on fabric.

First of all, it was used as a frieze on a plain cream window blind and then stencilled onto the same fabric as that used for the curtains to make tie-backs. The tie-backs were piped in red to match the braid which outlined the otherwise plain curtains. A most effective treatment, which completely changed the look of the kitchen for a very modest cost.

It is worth mentioning that when putting a design onto a window blind the first thing to do is to make sure that the first stencil is dead centre. Measure to the centre of the blind, measure to the centre of the stencil and line up the two centres. Of course it also helps if the rest of the design fits neatly into the spaces left. Even if you have to finish, say, halfway through an apple, the complete design will still look alright so long as the central motif is in the centre of the blind because this is the point to which the eye will naturally be drawn.

Poppy

I am particularly fond of poppies and this design is based on the shape of one I saw hand-painted on some china. Obviously the painted shape was much more subtle and detailed than any stencil could be, but I thought it would make the basis of a good stencil and experimented a great deal before settling on the shape shown here.

On page 11 you can see the design much enlarged and used eight times on a circular tablecloth. To achieve regularity the cloth was first folded in half, in half again and then once more. The crease lines gave the exact spacings needed and I measured from the bottom of the cloth to the bottom of the stem every time so that in each case the buds at the top of the design reached the edge of the table.

The same design, much reduced this time, was used to create the matching curtain tie-back shown in the centre of the photograph on page 10. A few extra simple leaves have been added to 'fill' out the depth of the tie-back but it could have been left just as it was.

Because I like the idea of needlework tie-backs I also stencilled it onto some tapestry canvas and worked it in wools to see how it would look. You can see the result on the left of the picture.

If you find the idea of cutting out the stamens rather daunting, do not forget that these could be added later using either a fine paintbrush or a special 'fabric' felt pen.

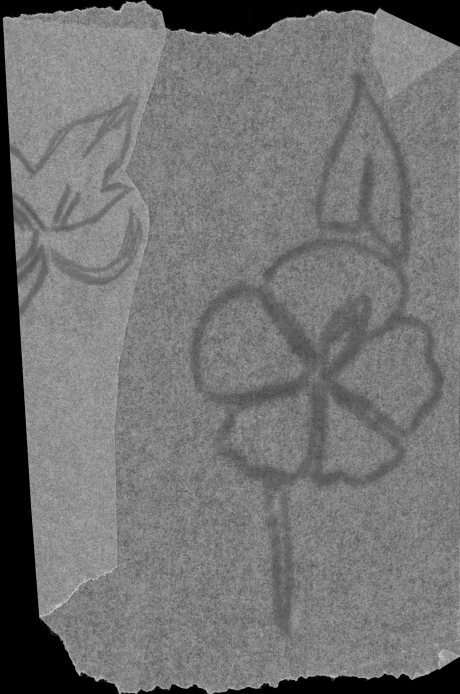

Iris

The shape of the Iris makes it an ideal stencilling subject and the one shown opposite is particularly useful for creating subtle colourings in the centre and around the edges of the flower head.

On the jacket of this book you will see that I have twice used it as a cushion cover to suit different room schemes. Both cushions have been stencilled onto raw silk, which has a wonderful texture.

To produce the cushion design I both enlarged and reduced the stencil shape and first worked out the design on squares of paper outlined to the finished cushion size I had decided upon. The different flower sizes add interest to the overall design, and by placing them at various angles it is not too obvious that the same design has been used over and over again.

When I was happy with the paper design I transferred the whole thing onto the raw silk, outlining it with a simple edging. The gold and yellow cushion was further emphasised with a deep gold piping and the violet and mauve cushion was simply quilted to give a more textured effect. In both cases I added a hand-painted darker green centre line to the leaves to add interest to the finished design.

Hibiscus

This design is based on the Australian Golden Hibiscus flower. It is such an extravagant-looking flower that at first it did not seem possible to reduce its shape to simple stencilled outlines. After looking carefully, it became obvious that if the bold stamen could be emphasised then the petals could take on simpler forms.

The result is shown opposite, and as I did not want to frighten new stencillers with complicated indentations and curves the basic petal shapes are quite simple. However, for the more experienced cutter I would suggest that these shapes could be made to look more interesting by adding more curves to the outside edges, sculpting them with the cutting knife.

This is a useful floral design because elements of it, such as the bud and leaf at the top, or just one of the serrated leaves could be used on their own. Imagine the whole design used to edge a tablecloth with the bud and leaf used in a random fashion over the rest of the cloth. Alternatively, the top bud and leaf could be combined with one of the leaves to make a complementary napkin.

Desert Rose

The Desert Rose is a delicately fragile flower which has somehow managed to adapt itself for survival in difficult desert conditions. It is similar to the English mallow in appearance, and an ideal shape for conversion into an elegant stencil.

As with the Hibiscus one of its most noteworthy features is the attractive stamen which has been given emphasis in this stencil. Again, if worried about your ability to cut the small circles, I would suggest that you fill these in with felt pen after stencilling the main design.

As a final touch, when the design has been stencilled, use a fabric felt pen to add dots of matching or contrasting colour around the stamen and slightly over the top petal to give a more three-dimensional effect.

Peony Flowerhead

This exuberant flower stencil is one that I have used over and over again.

I first used it to edge a throwover bedspread in striking deep rose shades. Because it was a very large bedspread intended for a double bed, I decided to make a circle of the design and place it in the centre of the bedspread so that the expanse of white was broken up and it looked more interesting.

The best way of placing a central motif on something like a large bedspread is to actually put the article in place on the bed. It is then much easier to see where the design would look best, as a certain amount of the overall depth will be taken up by the allowance needed for pillows – a central motif on a flat piece of fabric is not necessarily central when in place on a bed!

Next, measure the width of the bed from edge to edge, mark the half-way point with tailors chalk. Then, using the chalk mark as a guide, measure from beneath the pillows to the foot of the bed and again mark the half-way point with chalk. Where the two chalk marks cross is the centre of the design area and you can work outwards from this in a square, circle, or whatever central shape you have decided upon.

51

Wren

This is the stencil which I used to produce all the effects which you can see on pages 12 and 13.

If you find the thought of cutting the wing and tail feathers rather daunting use a pencil to link various sections together and then cut them out as one. As long as you follow the general direction of the various feathers this should work well.

You can see from the examples on pages 12 and 13 that I have both enlarged and reduced this design to suit various needs and you should bear this in mind with all the stencils in this book, for they can all be reduced or enlarged to create the effect *you* want.

Emu Fairy Wren

This design is based on the Australian Emu Fairy Wren. It came about because a client had asked for a small, interesting bird design to decorate fabric in her conservatory which contained several prettily-shaped bird cages.

Whilst I like to produce designs based on real-life subjects I do feel that the shape and the composition of any stencil is more important than strict accuracy. With this in mind I decided to go for an interestingly-shaped bird which would make a lively stencil..

Looking through several books on birds I discovered that the Australian wrens were many and varied, with wonderfully coloured plumage and spectacular tail feathers. Greatly enthused, I produced four different stencil designs and this is the one the client chose. It looked wonderful on the blinds in the conservatory, and when used in various sizes stencilled onto a round tablecloth and cushion covers.

Parakeet

The marvellous thing about parakeets is that they come in a vast variety of colours and it was for this reason that I thought it would be fun to design a parakeet stencil to use in a child's bedroom.

Using simple calico curtains as a base, the paraqueet was stencilled in the bright primary colours of red, blue, yellow and green. Sometimes the head would be scarlet with blue back and green breast feathers. The next one would have a blue head, scarlet breast and green back, and so on and so on. The only thing all the stencils had in common was bright yellow beaks and feet. Again, a unique pair of curtains that no manufactured design could emulate.

Bunch of Grapes

Grapes are always a popular motif, and this particular bunch can be reduced and enlarged to be used in many ways.

This stencil was originally designd to decorate squab cusions used in a conservatory which had an old and splendid vine growing along one wall and stretching along the roof. Some of the cushions were stencilled in various shades of purple and plum, some in lime greens and yellows, and some in a mixture of the two. This added an element of interest and individuality to the various chairs, and was achieved simply

Round and oval shapes can be quite difficult to cut out at first but the technique comes with growing confidence. Any jagged edges can be tidied up afterwards with the craft knife. The thing to remember is try and keep the tip of the knife in the piece to be cut out and move the paper around it. This will produce a much smoother line rather than trying to twist your wrist around the curves.

Cornucopia

This stencil was originally designed to decorate the dining room wall in a well-known Devon restaurant, and it looked particularly appropriate over a sideboard laden with delicious puddings and luscious fruit.

The owners liked the motif and asked me if I could reproduce it on canvas so that it could be worked to make complementary cushions. Although I did not realise it at the time, this was really the beginning of my needlework range.

Many stencils can be adapted to make a piece of needlework, and can be finished in different ways. On page 9 you can see the Cornucopia stencilled onto tapestry canvas and beneath it a complementary Fruit Bowl design – also used in the restaurant – worked with the background left untouched. This is because it is intended to be a wall-hanging and by leaving the background unworked the piece takes on a three-dimensional effect, especially when surrounded by a sympathetic mount and frame.

As you can see, the stencil 'ties' have been ignored and the wool taken right over them. Often two differently coloured threads of wool have been used to add interest and texture to the various leaves and fruit. Perhaps this will inspire you to turn some of the other designs in this book into a piece of needlework!

Peacock

This much-reduced peacock stencil is the one which I used on the large screen shown on pages 6 and 7.

As you can see, it is quite a complicated stencil to cut. However, when it is enlarged the wing and tail 'feathers' are much easier to cut around and the narrow lines linking the 'eyes' on the tail can easily be put in with a fabric felt pen.

It is a very adaptable design and gives one the opportunity of using many colours. It is also an ideal design for toning with any overall room scheme as the various elements can be coloured to pick up the shades used in, say, the curtains or the sofa fabrics.

Of course it does not have to be enlarged at all, it will look equally good on curtains and sheers, or to decorate a round tablecloth in the same manner as the poppy design shown on page 11.